The turnpike road to people's hearts, I find,
Lies through their mouths or I mistake mankind.
John Wolcot

from The Boke of Curtasye
- Do not stuff mouth with bread
or you will look like an ape
- Do not slurp soup
- Do not pat the dog
- Do not spit in the basin
when washing hands,
especially if a prelate is present.
Anon. Published by William Caxton 1460

Canapé - a sandwich cut into twenty-four pieces.
Bill Rose

The Dodocorp Underwater Research Team looking for some red herrings

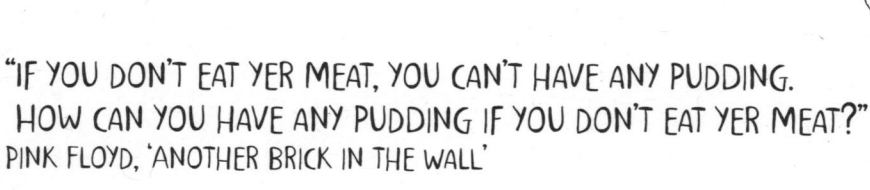

"IF YOU DON'T EAT YER MEAT, YOU CAN'T HAVE ANY PUDDING.
HOW CAN YOU HAVE ANY PUDDING IF YOU DON'T EAT YER MEAT?"
PINK FLOYD, 'ANOTHER BRICK IN THE WALL'

Punching the air is not just for sportsmen. Accountants do it when the figures add up; others do it when they get a mortgage or complete the Telegraph crossword. I have seen people do it when their home-made mayonnaise does not curdle.
Oliver Pritchett
The Dogger Bank Saga: Writings 1980-95

If Leekes you like, but do their smell dislike,
Eat Onyons, and you shall not smell the Leeke.
If you of Onyons would the scent expelle
Eat Garlicke that shall drown the Onyon's smell.
From The Philosophers' Banquet 1635

There, gleaming on the shiny black straw, was a scattering of crumbs, crumbs from a sponge cake, the kind of thing you would expect to find on the hat of a person who had stood on their head to have tea.
PL Travers
Mary Poppins Comes Back 1935

He was a bold man that first ate an oyster.
                        Jonathan Swift

Family gathers
to share good noise and good food.
Gratitude abounds.
Richelle E. Goodrich

Mozzarella and artichoke salad with pumpkin seeds arrived with the seeds still in their shells, as your parrot would expect them to be served.
A.A. GILL, (RESTAURANT REVIEW)

The trouble with eating Italian food is that five or six days later you're hungry again.
GEORGE MILLER

Are you the Salmon, Madam?

No, I'm a hungry soul with an empty place, waiting for someone to fill it.

IF WE'RE NOT MEANT TO HAVE MIDNIGHT SNACKS,
THEN WHY IS THERE A LIGHT IN THE FRIDGE?
ANON

Christmas was close at hand, in all his bluff and hearty honesty; it was the season of hospitality, merriment, and open-heartedness; the old year was preparing, like an ancient philosopher, to call his friends around him, and amidst the sound of feasting and revelry to pass gently and calmly away.
Charles Dickens

Mother: It's broccoli, dear.
Child: I say it's spinach, and the hell with it.
E.B. White; cartoon caption from New Yorker 8 December 1928

Food probably has a very great influence on the condition of men. Wine exercises a more visible influence, food does it more slowly but perhaps just as surely. Who knows if a well-prepared soup was not responsible for the pneumatic pump or a poor one for a war?

Georg Christoph Lichtenberg 1742-99

Part of the secret of success in life is to eat what you like and let the food fight it out inside.
Mark Twain

Never eat
more than you can lift.
MISS PIGGY

asked if he liked vegetables...
I don't know. I have never eaten them...
No, that is not quite true. I once ate a pea.
Beau Brummell

Toujours strawberries and cream
Samuel Johnson, quoted by Mrs Thrale in her 'Anecdotes'

Epitaph

Here lies poor BURTON
He was both hale & stout;
Death laid him on his bitter bier,
Now in another world he hops about.

Too many cooks, in baking rock cakes,
get misled by the word 'rock'.
PG Wodehouse

The noblest of all dogs is the hot dog.
It feeds the hand that bites it.
Laurence J. Peter

The best number for a dinner party is two—
myself and a damn good head waiter.

Nubar Gulbenkian
Observer, 'Sayings of the Week', 19 December 1919

When I ask for a watercress sandwich,
I do not mean a loaf with a field
in the middle of it.
Oscar Wilde

I like rice. Rice is great when you're hungry and want 2000 of something.

Mitch Hedberg

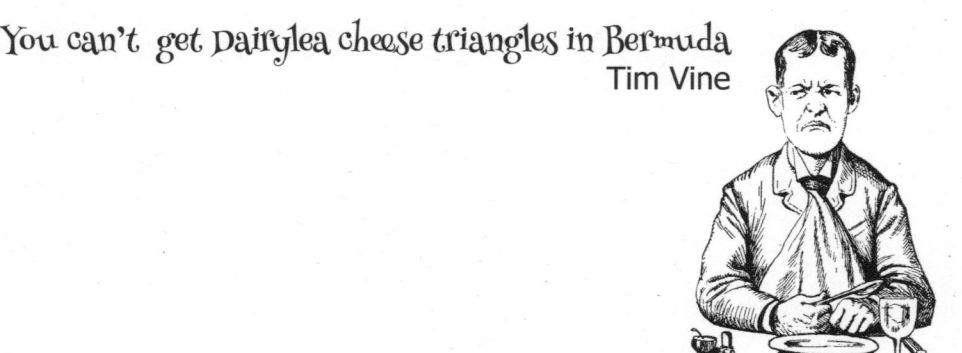

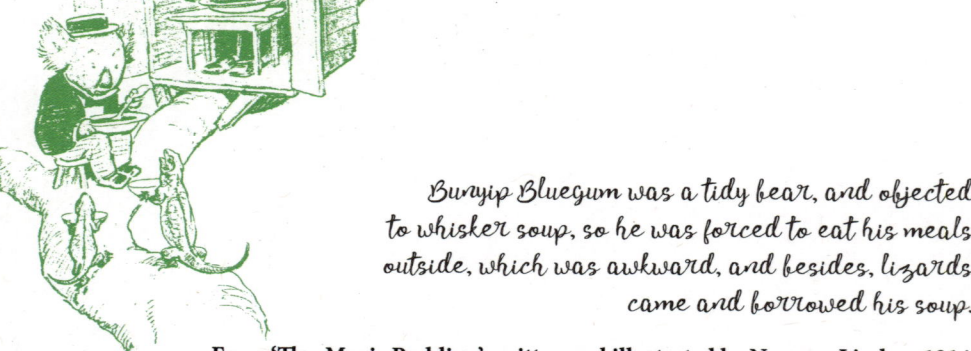

Bunyip Bluegum was a tidy bear, and objected to whisker soup, so he was forced to eat his meals outside, which was awkward, and besides, lizards came and borrowed his soup.

From 'The Magic Pudding', written and illustrated by Norman Lindsay 1914

"I propose a toast to mirth; be merry! Let us complete our course of law by folly and eating! Indigestion and the digest. Let Justinian be the male, and Feasting, the female! Joy the depths! Live, O creation! The world is a great diamond. I am happy. The birds are astonishing. What a festival everywhere! The nightingale is a gratuitous Elleviou. Summer, I salute thee!"
Victor Hugo, Les Misérables

 When I am in trouble, eating is the only thing that consoles me. Indeed, when I am in really great trouble, as anyone who knows me intimately will tell you, I refuse everything except food and drink.
Oscar Wilde
Algernon Moncrieff in 'The Importance of Being Earnest'

The mountain sheep are sweeter,
But the valley sheep are fatter;
We therefore deemed it meeter
To carry off the latter.
Thomas Love Peacock *Crochet Castle* 1831

Life is a combination of magic & pasta.
Federico Fellini

Hang your prune sauce, say I.
Oliver Goldsmith – Sir Charles Marlow in *She Stoops to Conquer* 1773

THINGS NOT TO BE FORGOTTEN AT A PICNIC
A stick of horseradish, a bottle of mint-sauce well corked, a bottle of salad dressing, a bottle of vinegar, made mustard, pepper, salt, good oil, and pounded sugar. If it can be managed, take a little ice. It is scarcely necessary to say that plates, tumblers, wine-glasses, knives, forks, and spoons, must not be forgotten; as also teacups and saucers, 3 or 4 teapots, some lump sugar, and milk, if this last-named article cannot be obtained in the neighbourhood. Take 3 corkscrews.
Isabella Beeton's Book of Household Management 1861

There is nothing so beautiful as the free forest. To catch a fish when you are hungry, cut the boughs of a tree, make a fire to roast it, and eat it in the open air, is the greatest of all luxuries.

Edmonia Lewis

Long as there is chicken and gravy
on your rice
Ev'rything is nice.
        Johnny Mercer "Lazybones" 1932

Sell a man a fish, he eats for a day.
Teach a man to fish, you ruin a
wonderful business opportunity.
Karl Marx (attrib).

A love of life, spaghetti and the odd bath in olive oil....
Everything you see I owe to spaghetti.

Sophia Loren

I am a man more dined against than dining.
Maurice Bowra, quoted in 'Summoned by Bells',
John Betjeman 1960

Let first the onion flourish there,
Rose among roots, the maiden-fair,
Wine-scented and poetic soul
Of the capacious salad bowl.
Robert Louis Stevenson

PUN GENTS

Indul gent

Overindul gent

I never see any home cooking.
All I get is the fancy stuff.
HRH The Duke of Edinburgh

Waitress, what on earth is this?
It's bean soup, sir.
Never mind what it's been. What is it now?

To make a good salad is to be a brilliant diplomatist — the problem is entirely the same in both cases. To know exactly how much oil one must put with one's vinegar.
Oscar Wilde

GRUB FIRST - THEN ETHICS.
Bertold Brecht

I scream
You scream
We all scream
For ice-cream

Anon. Collected in

A Treasury of American Folklore
BA Botkin 1944

"Let me see if Philip can
Be a little gentleman;
Let me see if he is able
To sit still for once at table"

Heinrich Hoffmann
Struwwelpeter 1848

If you're trying to create a company, it's like baking a cake. You have to have all the ingredients in the right proportion.
Elon Musk

I care not who hoes the lettuce of my country
if I can eat the salad!
F. Scott Fitzgerald

If there is a pure and elevated pleasure in this world it is a roast pheasant with bread sauce. Barn door fowls for dissenters but for the real Churchmen, the thirty-nine times articled clerk–the pheasant, the pheasant.

Sydney Smith

Red beans and ricely yours.
LOUIS ARMSTRONG, SIGNING OFF A LETTER

To fulfill a dream, to be allowed to sweat over lonely labour, to be given a chance to create, is the meat and potatoes of life. The money is the gravy.
Anon

Bread that must be sliced with an axe is bread that is too nourishing.
Fran Liebowitz

The embarrassing thing is that my salad dressing is out-grossing my films.
Paul Newman

Custard: a detestable substance produced by a malevolent conspiracy of the hen, the cow and the cook.
Ambrose Bierce

Then Bacchus and Silenus and the Maenads began a dance, far wilder than the dance of the trees; not merely a dance of fun and beauty (though it was that too) but a magic dance of plenty, and where their hands touched, and where their feet fell, the feast came into existence— sides of roasted meat that filled the grove with delicious smells, and wheaten cakes and oaten cakes, honey and many-colored sugars and cream as thick as porridge and as smooth as still water, peaches, nectarines, pomegranates, pears, grapes, straw-berries, raspberries—pyramids and cataracts of fruit.

C.S.Lewis *Prince Caspian*

I live on good soup, not on fine words.
Molière

There was an old Irish priest
Who lived almost wholly on yeast.
He said 'For 'tis plain
We must all rise again
And I'd rather get started at least!'
Anon
from the collection of Enid Buckley

I want someone to look at me the way
I look at chocolate cake.
Anon.

 Take away that pudding - it has no theme.
Winston Churchill, quoted in *The Way the Wind Blows: an Autobiography* by Lord Home 1976

'It's very easy to talk,' said Mrs Mantalini. 'Not so easy when one is eating a demnition egg,' replied Mr Mantalini; 'for the yolk runs down the waistcoat, and yolk of egg does not match any waistcoat but a yellow waistcoat, demmit.'

Charles Dickens
Nicholas Nickleby

Hors d'oeuvres have always a pathetic interest for me—they remind me of one's childhood that one goes through wondering what the next course is going to be like—and during the rest of the menu one wishes one had eaten more of the hors d'oeuvres.

Saki (H.H. Munro)

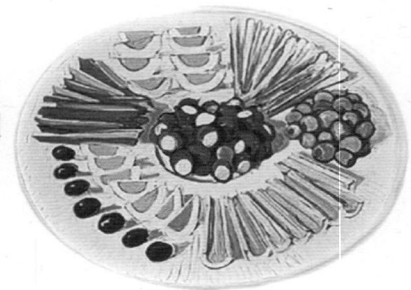

Fishes live in the sea, as men do on land: the great ones eat up the little ones.

Pericles

"YOU'LL NEVER MISS THE WATER"

Life is like asparagus... You eat the juicy bits first and by the time you get to my age, all you have left is a mouthful of chewed string.
                    Lord Dodo

Abstain from Beans
Pythagoras

Good apple pies are a considerable part
of our domestic happiness.
Jane Austen in a letter to Cassandra Austen 1815.

Training is everything: cauliflower is nothing but a cabbage with a college education.
Mark Twain

When dinner is finished, the dessert is placed on the table, accompanied with finger-glasses... The hostess, whose behaviour will set the tone to all the ladies present, will merely wet the tips of her fingers, which will serve all the purposes required. The French and other continentals have a habit of gargling the mouth; but it is a custom which no English gentleman should, in the slightest degree, imitate.
Mrs Beeton's Book of Household Management 1859

I've learnt to spell hors d'oeuvres
And it grates on many people's nerves
Warren Knox

You cannot eat a bun from the middle.
Anon. Chinese proverb, quoted in *A Gentleman's Commonplace Book*, John G. Murray 1996

ACCORDING TO THE SPANISH PROVERB, FOUR PERSONS ARE WANTED TO MAKE A GOOD SALAD: A SPENDTHRIFT FOR OIL, A MISER FOR VINEGAR, A COUNSELLOR FOR SALT AND A MADMAN TO STIR IT ALL UP.

JOHN GERARD

*Serenely full, the epicure would say,
Fate cannot harm me, I have dined today.*

Sydney Smith, letter to RH Barham 1841

Recipe for a Peaceful Disposition

A healthful & vigorous constitution, moderate exercise, a wholesome & odiferous air and a mind undisturbed with disappointed ambition or the anxious cares of avarice.

from The London Art of Cookery
by John Farley 1783